THE GREAT YELLOWSTONE FIRE

CAROLE GARBUNY VOGEL

AND

KATHRYN ALLEN GOLDNER

Sierra Club Books | Little, Brown and Company
San Francisco | Boston · Toronto · London

To our parents

First Paperback Edition
10 9 8 7 6 5 4 3 2 1
S C

Sierra Club Books/Little, Brown children's books are published by Little, Brown and Company (Inc.) in association with Sierra Club Books.

Published simultaneously in Canada by Little, Brown & Company (Canada) Limited

Printed in Hong Kong

Acknowledgments
The authors would like to thank the following people from the Public Affairs Office at Yellowstone National Park for their assistance: Joan Anzelmo, Mary Anne Davis, Kim Laubach, Sandra Robinson, and Amy Vanderbilt. The authors would also like to thank Golden LeFevre of TW Services, Inc., for his help.

Photo Credits
© Erwin and Peggy Bauer: 7 (bottom), 22, 23 (top right and bottom right), 29; Boise Interagency Fire Center: 10; © Robert Bower, Idaho Falls Post-Register: 1, 3, 23 (left); © Alan and Sandy Carey: 6, 7 (top), 8, 14 (right), 20, 21, 24, 25, 31; © Stephen M. Dowell, Bozeman Chronicle: 15, 16, 17 (left), 26 (right), 27; © Jeff Henry: 9, 14 (left); National Park Service: 11, 12, 17 (right), 18, 19, 26 (left), 28; Wyoming Travel Commission: 4, 5, 13, 30 (left and right).

Library of Congress Cataloging-in-Publication Data

Vogel, Carole Garbuny.
    The great Yellowstone fire / Carole Garbuny Vogel and Kathryn Allen Goldner. — 1st ed.
        p. cm.
    Summary: Describes the huge forest fires that burned almost one million acres of Yellowstone National Park in 1988 and the effects on the ecology of the forest there.
    ISBN 0-316-90522-4 (hc)
    ISBN 0-316-90249-7 (pb)
    1. Forest fires — Yellowstone National Park — Juvenile literature.
2. Fire ecology — Yellowstone National Park — Juvenile literature.
3. Yellowstone National Park — Juvenile literature. [1. Forest fires — Yellowstone National Park. 2. Fire ecology. 3. Ecology. 4. Yellowstone National Park. 5. National parks and reserves.]
I. Goldner, Kathryn Allen. II. Title.
SD421.32.Y45V64 1990
634.9'618'0978752 — dc20   89-29318

IN YELLOWSTONE NATIONAL PARK, heat and water escape from the earth into a land of mystery. Where volcanoes once erupted, strange creations of nature now bubble and hiss. Colorful, steaming pools dot fields of bunchgrass and sagebrush. Geysers gurgle and shoot columns of superheated water high into the air.

A dramatic fountain of steam and hot water shoots skyward from Castle Geyser, just one of about 10,000 geysers, hot springs, and other thermal features in Yellowstone.

Throughout the park, areas like Gibbon Meadow offer sunny, open spaces beside the dark pine forests.

Around these simmering landforms rise the rugged Rocky Mountains of Wyoming, Montana, and Idaho. Sharp gray peaks capped with snow tower above green forests. Streams and rivers tumble through deep gorges.

Lodgepole pine trees blanket much of Yellowstone. These trees grow tall and thin with few branches. In the dense forests, their tops mesh together, and little sunlight filters through. Open meadows and groves of spruce, fir, and aspen trees interrupt the pines.

◀ **Over millions of years, moving water carved out the Grand Canyon of the Yellowstone River.**

Yellowstone's patchwork of habitats provides homes for many kinds of animals. Near steaming geysers and hot springs, bison graze in open meadows. Moose and deer browse on tender shoots of cottonwood and willow. On steep mountainsides, golden eagles build nests on rocky ledges, and bighorn sheep traverse the jagged rocks. The rivers and lakes of the park provide food and nesting sites for trumpeter swans, white pelicans, and other water birds.

In 1872, the vast area known as Yellowstone was declared a national park to preserve its special landforms, wildlife, and wilderness for future generations to enjoy. The rules of the national park protect the animals from hunters and the trees from loggers. But no one can protect the forests from the forces of nature. As in ages past, summertime brings wildfire to Yellowstone.

An elk and her young calf share a quiet moment by a stream. Seven large herds of elk roam the meadows and forests of Yellowstone.

6

The variety of animal life in the park is remarkable, ranging from black bears like this little cub (top) to flocks of water birds such as the American white pelican (bottom).

In 1886, fourteen years after the formation of the park, Yellowstone officials declared fire the enemy. Although fire had been part of the wilderness for thousands of years, firefighters armed with axes and shovels were now sent to stamp out blazes. For many years, there was no effective way to combat flames in areas far from roads. After World War II, lookouts were stationed on mountaintops to watch for smoke, and smoke jumpers parachuted from airplanes into hard-to-reach places. Wildfires were extinguished as soon as possible.

After smoke jumpers began to parachute into wilderness areas, firefighting became much more effective.

Fallen trees, dead pine needles, and other natural litter continued to pile up on the forest floor. As the lodgepole forests aged, pine bark beetles attacked the trees, until thousands of dead and dying pines filled the forests. No major fires cleared away this buildup of fuel.

Over the years, as scientists learned more about forests, they discovered that fire is not the enemy. By clearing the land and releasing the minerals locked in dead wood, fire creates and maintains a variety of habitats. Like sunshine and rain, fire is necessary to the health of the wilderness.

In 1972, scientists convinced park officials to allow fire to play

Most wilderness fires are spotted from high atop mountain peaks. This fire lookout at Pelican Cone is one of four in Yellowstone.

its role in nature once again. Under the new policy, firefighters battled only blazes started by humans and those natural fires that threatened people or buildings. Precipitation in all seasons kept much of Yellowstone moist, so most natural fires died quickly.

In 1988, park officials expected another normal fire season. After a dry winter, spring precipitation was high. Fires ignited by lightning all fizzled out.

Then, in June, conditions changed. The air turned hot and dry, and practically no rain fell. Day after day, the sun beat down on Yellowstone. Lakes and streams shrank. In the meadows, grasses shriveled. In the forests, dead lodgepole pines and fallen branches became parched. Slowly, the landscape changed from lush green to withered brown.

In the summer of 1988, lightning started more than forty-five fires in Yellowstone—twice the usual number for one summer.

Thunderstorms rumbled across the park but brought no rain. Lightning ignited many small fires. Some died quickly, while others sprang to life. The fires burned unevenly, scorching here, singeing there. They leapfrogged through the forests, leaving patches of trees and ground cover untouched. Pushed along by dry summer winds, the fires grew.

Just over the park boundary in Targhee National Forest, woodcutters accidentally started another fire. The flames quickly spread into Yellowstone. Firefighters battled this blaze and several others that threatened buildings, but they could not stop the fires.

10

By midsummer, almost 9,000 acres of Yellowstone's 2.2 million acres had burned. Fires raged through forests that had taken hundreds of years to grow. No rain was expected for weeks, and officials were worried. On July 15, they decided to fight all new natural blazes. Within a week, they began to battle all existing ones, as well. Yet the fires continued to spread.

Fire consumed dead leaves and fallen logs and ignited living shrubs and trees.

Wildfires usually burn more slowly at night, then rev up with the heat of day. But in the summer of 1988, dry night winds blew down from high ridges, fanning the blazes. Day and night, ground fires crackled through dead pine needles, branches, and logs, blackening the forest floor. In some places, they scorched the bases of trees but left the tops green. In other areas, the ground fires burned hotter and toasted needles in the crowns of the trees a dusty rust color.

The hottest flames clawed up the trunks of large trees. Treetops ignited in seconds, and smoke poured into the sky. Lodgepole pines burst apart, hurling bits of glowing wood through the air. These tiny blazing embers landed on dry branches or grass and kindled spot fires far ahead of the fire fronts.

Advancing as much as five to ten miles a day, the fires hopscotched through the wilderness. Among the burned forests and meadows, they left unburned areas of green trees and brown grass.

The landscape became a patchwork of colors that reflected the pattern of burn. Scorched brown trees separate the areas blackened by the hottest flames from the green areas left untouched.

◄ **Hot flames leapt up tinder-dry tree trunks.**

From sunup to sunset and into the night, nearly 9,500 firefighters from all parts of the country battled the blazes. Many of these men and women prepared firebreaks. They cleared strips of ground of everything that could burn. Sometimes they scraped the land with hand tools; at other times, they detonated explosives or set small backfires. They sprayed trees and buildings with water or fire-retardant foam and snuffed out spot fires.

To fight remote blazes, firefighters hiked into the backcountry. Smoke jumpers parachuted in. Sometimes fire crews dropped water or fire retardant onto the blazes from helicopters and airplanes.

Yet the fires defied everyone's best efforts. Blazes subdued by water or retardant leapt back to life. Small fires grew and joined with bigger fires. Flames skipped over prepared firebreaks, roads, and rivers. One blaze even jumped the Grand Canyon of the Yellowstone River. By mid-August, experts agreed that only a change in weather could stop the fires.

Firefighters tried every known technique to control the blazes. On the roads, fire engines often shared the smoky landscape with animals trying to keep out of the fire's way (left). In the roadless wilderness, planes dropped pink fire retardant to smother the flames (right).

14

**When wind conditions permitted, firefighters lit small backfires that burned
toward the main blazes, clearing away the fuel.**

Some exhausted firefighters labored for thirty days in a row without a break. In the backcountry—grizzly bear territory—they had to sleep on the ground in small tents.

But the forecast for hot, dry weather remained unchanged. On August 20, the day that would be called Black Saturday, gale-force winds fanned every blaze in the park. Flames rampaged through forests and meadows. Smoke billowed high into the sky, and gray ash rained down.

Powerless, firefighters could only stand and watch while fire consumed another 160,000 acres. More of Yellowstone was blackened on this one day than in the previous 116 years. The amount of burned area in the park had doubled.

In late summer, fires inside and outside Yellowstone whipped toward several towns neighboring the park. Flames threatened many buildings inside Yellowstone, as well. Weary firefighters battled the blazes for twelve to fourteen hours a day.

Despite the raging fires, many people refused to cancel their vacations. They came to see the smoke, the wildlife, and the world's most famous geyser, Old Faithful.

◄ **Sometimes firefighters could only look on helplessly as fires raged out of control.**

Close to Old Faithful stands the rustic Old Faithful Inn, built in stagecoach days from logs, shingles, and stone. When it was completed in 1904, the inn and a cluster of buildings stood alone amid the geysers. Today, the inn is but one of many buildings — stores, gas stations, other lodges — that make up Old Faithful Village.

During the dry days of early September 1988, fire burned toward the famous geyser and the wooden structures of the nearby village. On the morning of September 7, officials began to evacuate tourists and workers from the area. Most people cooperated, but a few refused to leave.

Seemingly oblivious to billowing smoke, a group of tourists waited for Old Faithful to erupt on schedule.

At 2:00 P.M., the wind gathered speed. Beyond a nearby ridge, flames danced in the treetops. Lodgepole pines pitched and swayed, and the smell of burning trees filled the air. As the blaze swept up the far side of the ridge, fire-engine crews drenched buildings with water or fire-retardant foam. Other firefighters turned on a sprinkler system at the edge of the village complex.

At 3:30, Old Faithful erupted. Minutes later, a wall of flames whipped over the ridge. Roaring like jets in takeoff, the fire rolled down the forested hillside. Trees ignited like torches. Clouds of smoke turned the sky orange . . . then bronze . . . then gray . . . .

Fire roared over a ridge in Upper Lamar Valley; a similar blaze approached Old Faithful. ▶

On September 7th, fire whipped down the hillside behind Old Faithful Village. The wind shifted, and suddenly flames headed toward the buildings.

Within minutes, fire engulfed a pine grove on the edge of the village. Cabins burst into flames. A truck burned and then exploded.

Park employees, reporters, and the few remaining visitors fled toward the relative safety of the parking lot around Old Faithful Inn. Smoke stung their eyes and throats. Hot coals pelted their backs and flew past their heads.

Fire crews sprayed the buildings as pumper trucks raced through the smoky village to extinguish spot fires. A rooftop sprinkler system flooded the shingles of the inn.

20

Minutes later, the fire reached the edge of the village. Engulfed in thick smoke and threatened by blazing embers, historic Old Faithful Inn was saved by a rooftop sprinkler system.

For more than an hour, the fire roared and crackled around the village. It jumped a barren stretch of land and continued to burn on the other side. Bypassed by the flames, Old Faithful geyser erupted right on schedule. Its spray mixed with the ash-laden air and drained away, a gray slurry.

When the smoke finally cleared, twenty structures on the outskirts of the village — mostly cabins and storage buildings — lay in smoldering ruins. But Old Faithful Inn and the other major buildings survived unharmed.

Months after flames had swept through, pockets of fire still smoldered in the trunks and roots of trees.

For three more days, fires roared through Yellowstone. Then, on September 11, a light snow fell. In the following days, moist fall weather slowed the flames, and the thick smoke began to break up and drift away. Though fires smoldered for many weeks, the major battle was over.

All through the summer, while the forests and meadows were burning, the animals followed their instincts, and most survived. Small meadow animals, such as squirrels and mice, hid from flames in underground burrows. Large mammals, such as bears and elk, seemed to sense the movement of the fires and wandered away.

22

Once the flames had passed, wildlife quickly returned to the burned sites. Insects fed on charred trees, and birds snapped up the insects. Squirrels and chipmunks scrounged for seeds. Hawks and owls hunted the small animals that had lost their hiding places.

In moist sites, new plant growth soon poked through the blackened earth, but the nourishing green shoots grew too sparsely to feed all the animals. Already lean from grazing on drought-stricken land, deer, bison, and elk could not build up thick fat reserves. They faced a difficult winter.

In recently burned areas, elk licked the ash for minerals (left); squirrels and owls searched for food in the charred forest (right). During the summer of 1988, nearly one-half of Yellowstone was touched by flames.

**Coyotes and other scavenging animals feasted on elk and deer
that perished during the harsh winter after the fire.**

By late November, heavy snows chilled Yellowstone. The seven previous winters had been mild, and few large mammals had died. Now, bigger-than-normal herds of elk, deer, and bison competed for a smaller-than-normal food supply. Many of these grazing animals began to starve. During storms and cold snaps, hundreds of the very young and the very old died. Their frozen bodies provided food for bears, coyotes, and bald eagles.

More animals than usual migrated into neighboring forests and towns in search of food. Outside Yellowstone, park rules did not protect the animals. Hunters killed far more elk and bison than in previous years.

◄ **Winter snows finally snuffed out the last of the fires of 1988.**

In the spring, melting snow moistened the parched ground of Yellowstone. Unharmed roots of blackened grasses and shrubs absorbed the water. Countless seeds that had survived in the soil swelled with moisture. Many other seeds drifted into the burned areas from nearby patches of healthy vegetation. Together with sunlight and the nutrients from burned wood and underbrush, the water triggered an ancient cycle of regrowth.

Grasses sprouted and wildflowers bloomed. Aspens grew new branches and leaves. Berry bushes blossomed and thrived. Freed from their cones by the fires, lodgepole pine seeds germinated. Among the new flowers and grasses, tiny green pine trees dotted the ash.

The elk and bison that survived the harsh winter fattened up on the rich new growth. Bears feasted on berries, and porcupines nibbled fresh, green grass. Squirrels and mice flourished on the abundance of new seeds. Woodpeckers in search of insects pounded holes in dead trees, creating nesting sites for songbirds.

Temperature-sensitive lodgepole pinecones burst open in the heat of the fire, scattering their seeds (left). In moist areas, grasses began to sprout just days after fire swept through (right).

26

A bison grazed on tender new grasses, her calf at her side, as springtime brought renewal to the park.

Within a few growing seasons, a carpet of grasses, flowers, shrubs, and tiny tree seedlings will transform most of Yellowstone's burned areas into lush meadows. These new meadows will provide a bounty of food for the animals.

As the bushes and shrubs continue to grow, they will shade the sun-loving plants beneath them. Gradually the grasses and flowers will die. The lodgepole pine seedlings will poke above the other plants; in a decade, they will be three to four feet high.

Eventually wind will knock down most of the blackened trees. Along streams and rivers, the toppled trunks will support the banks. They will break up the current and improve the habitat for trout and other fish.

The young pines will grow taller and taller, and within forty years new lodgepole forests will replace the forests that burned. The high branches of the pines will grow together and prevent sunlight from reaching the forest floor. In the dim understory, the bushes and shrubs will die; they will no longer provide berries and shoots for hungry animals. The new dense stand of trees will contain little variety of food. Most animals will move on to new meadows created by more recent fires.

Amid the charred ruins of an old forest, healthy new lodgepole pine seedlings are off to a good start.

◄ **After the fires, spring wildflowers bloomed abundantly in the sunny open spaces of the park.**

Geologic wonders such as Morning Glory Pool (left) and Minerva Terrace at Mammoth Hot Springs (right) are the work of volcanic forces even more powerful than wildfire.

Summer wildfires have been changing the landscape of Yellowstone for at least 12,000 years. Most of the time, fires burn relatively small areas and alter the landscape only slightly. But every 250 to 400 years, a combination of drought, strong winds, and fuel buildup produces colossal wildfires that sweep through the aging lodgepole forests and change the landscape more significantly.

Below the surface of Yellowstone, forces far more powerful than wildfire have been shaping the land for millions of years—the forces of volcanism. Long ago, violent volcanic eruptions helped sculpt the mountains and plateaus of this region. Today, volcanic fires still simmer in the form of hot, melted rock two miles underground. The heat from this rock fuels the park's geysers, fumaroles, mudpots, and hot springs.

Someday far in the future, volcanoes will again erupt at Yellowstone. As in the distant past, these underground fires will alter the pattern of mountains and plateaus.

Much sooner, massive wildfires will again roar through Yellowstone. As in the summer of 1988, these surface fires will spark the renewal of meadows and forests.

Lovely meadows and forests like these at Hayden Valley display Yellowstone's timeless beauty. ▶